15 Marketing Words that will Make Your Clients Pay Attention to You

John Di Lemme

15 Marketing Words that will Make Your Clients Pay Attention to You
Copyright © 2015 John Di Lemme

Di Lemme Development Group, Inc.
931 Village Boulevard Suite 905-366
West Palm Beach, Florida 33409-1939
(561)847-3467
www.LifestyleFreedomClub.com

All rights reserved. No part of this book may be used or reproduced by any means, graphics, electronic, or mechanical, including photocopying, recording, taping or by any information storage retrieval system without the written permission of the author, John Di Lemme. Please contact Team@LifestyleFreedomClub.com to request permission to use quotes from this material.

This book is designed to provide competent and reliable information regarding the subject matters covered. However, it is sold with the understanding that the author is not engaged in rendering legal, financial, or other professional advice. Laws and practices often vary from state to state and if legal or other expert assistance is required, the services of a professional should be sought. The author specifically disclaims any liability that is incurred from the use and/or application of the contents of this book.

ISBN: 978-1-329-95478-6

John Di Lemme
High-End Business Consultant & Strategic Business Coach

In September 2001, John Di Lemme founded Di Lemme Development Group, Inc., a company known worldwide for its role in expanding the personal development industry. As President and CEO, John strives for excellence in every area of his business and believes that you must surround yourself with a like-minded team in order to stay on top of your game.

In addition to building a successful company, John has changed lives around the globe as an international, elite speaker that has spoken in over five hundred venues. Over the past fourteen years, he has shared the stage with the best of the best including Rich Devos, Denis Waitley, Jim Rohn, and Les Brown only to name a few. This is truly an amazing feat for someone that was clinically diagnosed as a stutterer at a very young age and told that he would never speak fluently. John's teachings have also been featured on Fox Small Business, Inc. Magazine, HSN *(Home Shopping Network),* CNBC, and in many other media outlets.

John truly believes that everyone needs personal development to reach their full potential in life, and his determination to reach all forms of media with his motivational marketing messages has catapulted his career. John has produced over four hundred fifty products and is an accomplished author of thirteen books including his best-selling book, "ABCs of Millionaire Marketing." As a High-End Business Consultant and Strategic Business Coach, John's students include doctors, lawyers, realtors, entrepreneurs, consultants, CEOs of million dollar companies, and various other occupations that are thriving in a so-called poor economy. John's success with his students has made him one of the most highly sought after business coaches in the world.

John's passion is to teach others how to live a champion life despite the label that society has placed on them. Through his books, audio/video materials, sold-out live seminars, numerous television interviews, intensive training boot camps, weekly tele-classes, Strategic Business Coaching, Closing & Marketing University, Millionaire Affirmation Academy, Motivation Plus Marketing Podcast, Channel for Success, and Lifestyle Freedom Club memberships, John has made success a reality for thousands worldwide.

Contact John's Elite Team to discover how you can book John to speak at your next event and learn more about his products and services. Call/Text (561) 847-3467 or Email Team@LifestyleFreedomClub.com

I am excited about this book, because it is literally the transcript of one of my most listened to marketing teachings over the past 15+ years. Throughout the book, you will see bolded text "Coaching Students" and "John." This is the actual interaction between me and my coaching students at the live event. How awesome is that!

Now, get ready to immerse yourself in some great marketing wisdom!

John Di Lemme

15 Marketing Words That Will Make Your Client Pay Attention to You

John: Welcome to the July DVD of the Month Marketing teaching for the Lifestyle Freedom Club. I do want to warn you. Warning: this teaching is being recorded at the 3-Day Strategic Coaching Student-Only mastermind event. Has it been intense in here, guys?

Coaching Students: Yes!

John: Now let my Coaching Students Give the Warning.

Coaching Students: Warning. What you're about to hear may affect your finances and may affect your life, because my life is changed forever. Now it's your decision time. So, get ready. Pay attention to my coach.

John: We did that warning because I want to teach probably a little stronger than normal on a message that goes out around the world. You may be listening to this a year from now, two years from now. This is the July 2015 DVD of the Month, titled "15 Marketing Words That Will Make Your Client Pay Attention to You."

When people pay attention to you, the trust process begins. How do you pay attention? You listen. If someone says, "Can you pay attention to me, please?" that means they want you to listen to them. You are going to hear some great stories, which is exciting. We have some of my top guns from around the country here live today. How awesome is this event?

Coaching Students: Awesome!

John: It's just a fabulous event. I'm telling you right now. When we put the power on this room, we assume that the electric bill has been paid for and that the outlet works. I have to assume that you're fully motivated: your morning miracle preparation is down, you have no useless relationships in your life, and you release the ego, you release your stubbornness, and you're totally focused. I'm under the assumption that that is occurring because without that, you'll never really be able to maximize marketing.

One time, I came into one of the events here and only one electrical outlet worked. We knew that these other outlets worked, because we've been here a zillion times. I also know all of you can produce record-breaking results in business. But we live in a very distracted, disorganized, and multi-tasking society.

Since we're in a distracted, multi-tasking society, the only way your customers can hear how their lives can benefit from you is when they pay attention to you. I'm going to be teaching this message from one of my top marketing books is "57 Must Use Words in Every Piece of Marketing You Do for Your Business."

Absolutely FREE *57* Must Use
Marketing Words for You!
www.FreeMarketingWords.com

I want you to write down "every piece." What "every piece" means is there are components of marketing. A lot of people think marketing is a website or a brochure.

Marketing is every piece, meaning when you open your mouth and you respond to a phone call, that's marketing. When you're replying to an e-mail, it's the words you type. I believe in a dialogue/quick-conversation e-mail. I don't believe that e-mail should be in the form of a letter. How many of you respond to e-mails on your phones? It's just about the entire room – 90%. This is why when I say "dialogue e-mail," I mean very short, sweet, and right to the point.

The days of long e-mails are over because you're on your phone. You're in the restroom, you're in the fitness center, you could be on in between church services. We have to realize that every piece of marketing, meaning every verbal communication on the phone, every e-mail communication, and obviously every flyer, brochure, and marketing piece you use – everything you do for your business is marketing. I want you to understand that. It's not a website, and it's not just an electronic app. People get so confused about what marketing is.

In this book, I'm going to pick the top 15 words from my book, 57 Must Use Words in Every Piece of Marketing You Do for Your Business. Now, let's get started…

Absolutely FREE *57* Must Use
Marketing Words for You!
www.FreeMarketingWords.com

6

Word #1: Dissatisfied

This is Word #20 in the *57* Must Use Words in Every Piece of Marketing You Do for Your Business book.

This is a guaranteed home run. How can you add "dissatisfied" into your marketing?

"It sounds as if you're dissatisfied with where you're at in life right now."

"Since you invested in this marketing DVD, it looks as if you're dissatisfied with your marketing. Tell me more about your dissatisfaction."

When you use the word "dissatisfaction" to a potential client, customer, consumer, or patient, you know that there's dissatisfaction there, but you have to dialogue it to them. You have to say, "It sounds as if you're dissatisfied." Or you can use it in your direct headline, your subject line: "Are you currently

Absolutely FREE *57* Must Use
Marketing Words for You!
www.FreeMarketingWords.com

dissatisfied with…?" It's a home-run. The more you use that, the more conversation you have with your clients. When someone sees the word "dissatisfied" with your niche and with your market, they're going to respond back. You're going to get their attention on just how bad they have a relationship with your specific niche. When you say "dissatisfied" and they pay attention to it and are listening to you, that means it's time for you to fill in the blanks, implement, and then share with them how you can go from dissatisfaction to complete satisfaction.

"When you make a decision today to grab a hold of the products and services I offer, you will go from complete dissatisfaction to incredible lifetime satisfaction."

Start using those words in your dialogue. Start to speak and understand those words. We're converting someone from dissatisfaction to satisfaction. Plus it grabs their attention instantly!

Word #2: Frustrated

This is Word #48 in the *57* Must Use Words in Every Piece of Marketing You Do for Your Business book.

This is dissatisfaction's cousin. When someone is dissatisfied, they're most likely frustrated. When someone is dissatisfied with a service, they're frustrated with the results they're searching for. I want to give you this line, also: "Are you frustrated with the results you're looking for in…?" Fill the blank in. ""Are you frustrated with the results you're searching for, because based upon your dissatisfaction, you're probably super-frustrated."

Once a month, I host a South Florida Small Business Entrepreneur Mastermind Meetup. I know that every single person who is there, regardless if they stay or not, is a Michael Z. He met me at the Meetup and left early, but is now an Elite Coaching Student. I'm

Absolutely FREE *57* Must Use
Marketing Words for You!
www.FreeMarketingWords.com

focused on discovering another Michael Z. See the process there? I know that people enter this room, because they're dissatisfied or frustrated with their current success in business and they are looking for a mastermind group in South Florida.

South Florida is a sunny place for wacky, freak show wanna be coaches. Did I get my point across? California, Florida, and Arizona are in complete craziness. So I know when people walk through that door, I have a serious commitment to convert their dissatisfaction to complete satisfaction and to convert their frustration to complete focus.

So start to use the word "frustrated" more. When you talk to people, let them know what you are hearing them say.

"What I'm hearing from you, Sandra, is your frustration level. Tell me more about your frustration."

I want everyone to write that down.

"I want to hear more about your frustration with your level of success. Tell me more about your frustration with your real estate business, your acupuncture business, your construction company, your law firm, your courier company, your bookkeeping business, your telecom services, your professional services, your painting and renovation services, your networking marketing business." Those are all the businesses of champions here in the room.

"Tell me more about your frustration with your_____." Fill in the blank.

Can I tell you a little side-story, which is hysterical? Christie & I were in Turks and Caicos, and we rented a catamaran. It had sailing lessons with the rental, but I said, "I don't have to take them. I had a sailboat." We used to have a sailboat in Milford, Connecticut, it was a Sunfish. There were about ten of us, all crazy cousins, and we used to play football with between the boats. We would set goal lines and make up our own rules. We would go back and forth with the little Sunfish boats and play football. It was completely out of control.

My cousin Pete, from Home Shopping Network, is a good swimmer. My other cousin John is an incredible swimmer. We would be in the boats, jump in the water, swim across, and pull the centerboard out of the other boat. Once the centerboard is gone, you're done. You're just spinning around in circles. Then we would end up flipping over the boat. Boys will be boys! The boat said "Oops" on the bottom of it, so they could see it on the beach.

So back to the Turks and Caicos story. As you can see, sailing is in my blood. I definitely didn't think that I needed sailing lessons for our catamaran. You're always going to have the tourists who know everything! All of a sudden, we're out there and it's as windy as can be. What happens? The wind stopped.

Christie says, "Mr. Sailor, we're not moving." We're in the current and there's no wind. All of a sudden, here comes the guy in the boat to rescue us. Of course, I don't know how to say, "There's no wind" in Spanish. Christie said, "We're not going anywhere. Maybe he should tow us in." It was like a scene from a movie – two stranded wannabe sailors out there. How long did it take us to get in? Forever! My mindset was, "I'm not getting towed in by the boat. I'll just blow in the sail if I have to!" It was like an hour and a half to get in. I knew how to sail, but there was no wind.

We were talking about dissatisfied and frustrated. I was frustrated with that wind. Understand how powerful frustration can be as a motivator for your client to do believe in you and turn their frustration into satisfaction.

In our marketing realm, start to use these words more: "Are you frustrated in...? Are you dissatisfied with...? Tell

Absolutely FREE *57* Must Use
Marketing Words for You!
www.FreeMarketingWords.com

me more about your frustration." You create a behavioral pattern of that, which is a habit. You create a habit of that in your marketing – "Tell me more about your frustration" – and you're going to hear more, and you're going to learn more, and when you learn more about your clients, you can then start to implement what products people want.

How about my dad and Amazon? How eye opening is that? Let that sink a little bit. My dad is 85. He buys everything on Amazon. It's amazing. Just a handful of years ago, how many of you bought something on Amazon besides books? There are no hands going up. Right now, how many of you buy things way beyond books on Amazon? Look at this.

Jeff Bezos, for 15 years, was laser-focused on creating an iconic, world-changing business based upon one thing – dissatisfaction and frustration of the consumer – and look at it now. It's pretty amazing. Just about everything I have was purchased from Amazon.

Word #3: FREE

This is Word #49 in the *57* Must Use Words in Every Piece of Marketing You Do for Your Business book.

People want a free report. People want something for free. Give them a free report. Give them a free appetizer. Give them a free dessert. Those of you who have a restaurant, say, "Today and today only, the first 17 who come in for lunch get a free appetizer/ a free dessert."

Ask yourself a question. "What can I give away for free in my business to deepen a relationship?" "I will give you a free 30-minute presentation/a free 30-minute overview of the benefits of my product or service." People want something for free.

"For the first 17 people that call right now, you will get a FREE _____." Fill in the blank.

Absolutely FREE *57* Must Use
Marketing Words for You!
www.FreeMarketingWords.com

Give people something for free. FREE is a word that gets everyone's attention. When you use the word "free" in your marketing, put *FREE* in asterisks. It pops right out. When you do an e-mail, *FREE* is automatically bolded if you have Google mail. Those of you who do not have a Gmail address, I suggest you get one, because how many of you think Google will be in business ten years from now?

Coaching Students: Yes.

John: So when people Google you and you have a Gmail address through Google, that may come up in your Google search. Interesting, right? So it's very important. All of my e-mails are based in Gmail, even though it's John@LifestyleFreedomClub.com and Team@LifeStyleFreedomClub.com. But behind it, is Gmail address.

All of you know, I speak a lot in the marketing world about reports. Give away a free report that reveals "How

To..." Such as a free report on how not to be scammed by South Florida contractors, a free report on how to pressure wash your deck, a free report on 17 ways to get creative to finance your property, a free report on how to never use the microwave oven again and how bad it is for you and so on. Anyone who either responds to you, by calling or texting you, or by taking a report, is an interested lead who has an interest in the item you are offering.

For example, we talked about targeting a high-end market here in South Florida for one of my top clients, Mark of Excellence Construction. Our goal is tomail everyone in that development the article titled "The Eight Secrets on How Not to be Scammed by South Florida Contractors." Anyone who calls on that report has been or is concerned about being scammed by a South Florida contractor.

Absolutely FREE *57* Must Use Marketing Words for You!
www.FreeMarketingWords.com

If I've not said it ten times, I've said it a thousand times. Whatever email your customers respond to or whatever they call/text in on, that's what they want to know more about. That's an interested lead!

If there are 100 people, you give away a free report, and only one responds, who cares about the other 99? You focus on the person who's interested. That's why cold calling is completely useless. Buying leads are a waste of time. You find your market. You market to them. They respond. They're interested and you close them for the long term.
The word "free" is awesome. Make it a regular part of your marketing. Always remember, you want to be giving people FREE bonuses.

Word #4: Amazing Breakthrough

This is Word #27 in the *57* Must Use Words in Every Piece of Marketing You Do for Your Business book.

This will make your client pay attention to you. It's actually two words: "amazing breakthrough."

"In Phoenix, New York, there is an amazing breakthrough in customer service and real estate. We actually call you back within one second to 24 hours. We actually listen to what you want. We actually have repeat customers. We have people raving about us. You think I'm kidding? Come on in. Take a look at our amazing Wall of Fame that ranges from doctors to blue collar workers. Think I'm kidding? Come on in."

How awesome is that?

"There's an amazing breakthrough in South Florida. Scott Rothstein is a Ponzi scam artist who's away forever, but there is an attorney you can trust in South Florida by the name of Carol L. Grant. Here's a free report for you just in case you may be dissatisfied or frustrated with the trust level with your attorney."

See the process here? How many of you have increased your income to unexplainable numbers in the last year?

Coaching Students: All of their hands are raised.

How powerful is that? Interesting. Let me explain something to you. That's a sampling of my coaching students. My coaching students who I coach in my locker room are breaking records in business and marketing. It's just a fact. It all has to do with words and the way we develop their marketing. Interesting, right?

"An amazing breakthrough in construction in South Florida...I actually

have a license and people who recommend me. They're not fake testimonials from ten years ago."
You don't want your testimonials to look like an episode of "Welcome Back, Kotter." I was watching a so-called coach online the other day and in his YouTube video testimonial, I was waiting for the "Welcome Back, Kotter" music to come on. Let me be very direct. It looked like the people in the room were from the 1970s and 1980s. How many of you believe that that's probably not current? It's not current. When you visit my YouTube channel, my first intro video is one of my most recent mastermind events from last month. If someone doesn't have recent testimonials, don't listen to them!

"Amazing breakthrough" are serious words to use. One of my Elite Coaching Students, Michael Zapanta, has learned this first hand. He's a physical therapist who's actually in great shape, not on steroids, and truly cares about his patients and their wellbeing. However, people confuse a physical therapist and a trainer. One of the top reports that Michael Zapata wrote is about the difference between a personal trainer and physical therapist. There's a big difference between them. Michael doesn't walk around with his sleeves rolled up, jacked up on steroids, drinking creatine, taking amino acids, looking in the mirror going, "I'm a physical therapist." Interesting, right. That's a big difference.

Michael is professional and highly educated, and one of the greatest physical therapists in Florida. So who doesn't like that report he's written? The personal trainers who are jacked up on the juice. Who loves that report? The patients who want long-term results. Now, that is an amazing breakthrough!

Word #5: Straight Talk

This is Word #33 in the *57* Must Use Words in Every Piece of Marketing You Do for Your Business book.

"Let me give you the straight talk about…" You fill the blank in about what your business can people the straight talk about. It's simply the straight talk about what you or your business can do for your customers. Plain and simple. It's get to the point! Give me the straight talk about what you can do for your customers. That will get your customers to pay attention to you. People will ultimately respect you being straightforward without all of the fluff.

People instantly pay attention to you, when they hear you say, "Allow me to give you the straight talk about… It sounds as if you're dissatisfied, you're frustrated. Just because I love my customers, I want to give you a free report that will reveal to you how to experience the amazing breakthrough." See the orchestration of the *57* Must Use Words in Every Piece of Marketing You Do for Your Business book. This is literally the orchestration. I'm picking 15 today, but as you start to use the words, these are specific words to get people to pay attention to you.

"Let me give you the straight talk about how a lawyer should treat you." "Let me give you the straight talk about what a real network marketer acts like: a professional business person who treats it like a business and who cares about you." Interesting, right? That's the straight talk.

All you do is put the bullet points down and verbalize it – either through an email, report, or verbally you express what's going on in their mind and give them the straight talk about it.

Word #6: How To Stop

This is Word #41 in the *57* Must Use Words in Every Piece of Marketing You Do for Your Business book.

Whatever you believe your client's number one frustration or dissatisfaction is, just use that. We talk about dialogue. These are conversational words. "It sounds as if you want to discover how to stop…"

"It sounds as if, based upon your frustration and dissatisfaction, you want to learn how to stop the internal fear about _____." Fill in the blank.

"How to stop the worry factor about wondering if this networking marketing company is just a bunch of weirdos.'"

How many of you believe sometimes network marketing companies are full of weirdos? Hallie has been one of my top students in direct selling for 23 years.

Absolutely FREE *57* Must Use
Marketing Words for You!
www.FreeMarketingWords.com

One of the number one network marketers in America is in our room here today from Ohio. How awesome is Hallie? She's awesome.

We just have to address the reality: whatever you believe your consumer has to stop.

"How to stop the massive disorganization and really be able to trust a bookkeeper." Carolann is a bookkeeper.

Whatever you think your clients wants to stop, just add that in there. This is an ever increasing and ever developing belief structure.

Word #7: We Don't Cut Corners

This is Word #24 in the *57* Must Use Words in Every Piece of Marketing You Do for Your Business book.

This is one of my favorites. This is almost a go-to one for me constantly. "We are the Di Lemme Development Group, and we don't cut corners. We make sure you're fully satisfied with the product."

Your clients don't have to worry about the old sale and bail routine from your company. They know that you will be there for them before and after the sale and look forward to building a long-term, profitable relationship.

"Look, Adolfi Real Estate doesn't cut corners. We've been in business for over 40 plus years, and in the last year, we've had record-breaking success because we're servicing our local neighbors here in the marketplace like never before.

Absolutely FREE *57* Must Use
Marketing Words for You!
www.FreeMarketingWords.com

They love us because we don't cut corners."

Use this as dialogue. When you're speaking to somebody, say, "It sounds as if you've been to other acupuncturists who cut corners. Tom, tell me about why you feel like they've cut corners on your treatment." See the little words we're dropping in?

"Based upon your dissatisfaction, your frustration, tell me a little bit more because it sounds like you want to learn how to stop…" See the words?

There's a language of marketing. We're teaching long-term commitment here. I know there's no "L" in this teaching but the language of marketing is powerful words - less talking and more listening. That's the language of marketing. Use the right words that will trigger a response that you can then reply to and have your consumer, customer, client, or patient tell you basically what they're looking for, and you respond.

Word #8: Bonus

This is Word #17 in the *57* Must Use Words in Every Piece of Marketing You Do for Your Business book.

People will pay attention to you when you say the word "bonus."

"Today there's an absolutely FREE Bonus!"

The word "Bonus" has to be part of you. "Bonus" has to be part of your culture. Your business should be known for giving bonuses. We're known for bonuses. How many of you have got bonuses at this event? You get bonuses every time you turn around.
You have to be known in business for bonuses.

Bonuses don't have to be expensive. They have to be personal. You have to care about the person. We believe that all of you should give bonuses away.

Absolutely FREE *57* Must Use
Marketing Words for You!
www.FreeMarketingWords.com

Small pieces of artwork are great bonuses. You heard Dr. Ira share about it. He gives them away in his medical office, where the corporate employees have them on their desk and they enjoy them. How many of you give artwork away? You get great responses from people. They will not throw this out. They will remember who gave it to them.

Ask yourself this question, "What bonuses can I give away to a customer and/or potential customer today?"

Please write that down for your marketing language. All your cheap, broke friends who know nothing about business will not agree with you on this. But remember, they're your friends; they're not part of your marketing language.

Word #9: As a Matter of Fact

This is Word #19 in the *57* Must Use Words in Every Piece of Marketing You Do for Your Business book.

This is unique, because I'm going to give you a couple ways to use "As a matter of fact."

"As a matter of fact, you're right about..." Fill in the blank.

All of you know, Strategy #15 in my 17 Closing Strategies book is where I talk about "You're right about that." You're in agreement with your customers about them with their frustration and dissatisfaction.

"As a matter of fact, you're right about most medical doctors." Don't battle them and say, "You're a better doctor." Come into agreement first. Say, "As a matter of fact, you're right about most

lawyers. They get under my skin and annoy me too."
Don't defend people you don't know, because you know your customers.

"As a matter of fact, you're right about most realtors. They don't call you back. They don't care about you. They're chasing a sale."

"As a matter of fact, you're right about most people who do pressure washing, painting, deck cleaning, and minor repairs. They're really bad."

Follow this up with...

"But what you're going to find out when you make the decision to engage our service is that your dissatisfaction and frustration about _____ is going to disappear."

Word #10: Replace

This is Word #18 in the *57* Must Use Words in Every Piece of Marketing You Do for Your Business book.

When you replace frustration, what do you have? Satisfaction. When you replace lack of integrity, what do you have? Integrity. When you replace an unlicensed contractor with Mark of Excellence Construction, what do you have? A licensed contractor. So we have to use the word "replace" to show how your product or service will get rid of your customer's dissatisfaction and frustration.

What did Amazon do? Amazon has simply replaced everyone's buying habits with their company. Amazon didn't tell me to wear underarm deodorant or shaving cream. I was already using those things, but I don't buy it from CVS or Walgreens anymore.

Absolutely FREE *57* Must Use
Marketing Words for You!
www.FreeMarketingWords.com

I now get it from Amazon. Interesting, right?

Amazon didn't reeducate me about my product. Amazon satisfied my buying habit and replaced where I used to buy my products. That's the difference between focused marketing and trying to convince someone to buy or use a product. Let me repeat how HUGE this is for you to get a hold of in your marketing mindset. Amazon satisfied my buying habit. It's that simple!

Hallie's direct selling business is up thousands of percentages and is explosive. Yet we haven't even begun building her business! There are more dissatisfied people in the industry of networking marketing, because they haven't found a true professional business person. They're going to find Hallie and replace all the dissatisfaction in the industry of multi-level marketing with a professional leader. Interesting, right? That's the whole mindset of replacing.

Word #11: No Need to Say Any More

This is Word #25 in the *57* Must Use Words in Every Piece of Marketing You Do for Your Business book.

"You will understand why we are known for record-breaking testimonials. After you read them all, there will be no need to say any more."

"There will be no need to say any more about what we can provide for you."

These words are very effective to use when you get to a point in your marketing where there is a little bit of a debate of what you can do for your customer. Sometimes in business, you may go back and forth with some people over some questions or objections. These are closing, final words.

"Look, there's no need to say any more from our perspective. You let us know

Absolutely FREE *57* Must Use
Marketing Words for You!
www.FreeMarketingWords.com

about your level of dissatisfaction and frustration. Here's a boatload of testimonials. Whenever you're ready to achieve _____ (whatever results they want), you let us know."

You know they have the problem that you can solve, but they are still skeptical. You know they have the frustration and dissatisfaction that your service can solve. "There's no need to say any more." Those are words to use towards the end and go for the opening up of the relationship.

Word #12: Your Shortcut To...

This is Word #29 in the *57* Must Use Words in Every Piece of Marketing You Do for Your Business book.

"Your shortcut to sanity with attorneys."

"Your shortcut to massive integrity with a physical therapist."

"Your shortcut to feeling better than ever, healthier than ever, discovering and identifying a true acupuncturist who can change your life."

How many people want a shortcut? So tell them that. We know they want a shortcut, and they're going to pay attention. They're going to hear that.

"Your shortcut to finally discovering a home-based business that will give you the opportunity you've been searching for."

Absolutely FREE *57* Must Use
Marketing Words for You!
www.FreeMarketingWords.com

"This is your shortcut to _____.
You've found the right place."
See the process there? People naturally want a shortcut, so when we use those words, we get them to pay attention.

What's the title of this message? "15 Top Marketing Words that Will Make Your Client Pay Attention to You." I'm going to add it in, "and Ultimately Do Business with You" because that's the goal.

Word #13: Danger

This is Word #50 in the *57* Must Use Words in Every Piece of Marketing You Do for Your Business book.

"Danger in the _____." Fill in the blank.

"Just like there are Bernie Madoffs and Scott Rothsteins in the Ponzi scheme realm, there are people who are unethical and looking to take your money in the (insert your industry).

"Danger in the bookkeeping world."

"Danger in the real estate world."

"Danger in the construction world."

"Catch a Contractor" on Spike TV is one of the fastest growing reality shows. Why? Because everyone is trying to watch it to find out how to not be taken advantage by contractors. That's the

Absolutely FREE *57* Must Use
Marketing Words for You!
www.FreeMarketingWords.com

reason why the viewership is skyrocketing. They're learning from the host, Adam and Skip. They're learning how to not be victimized.

It all starts with, "I liked him. They were nice people. They were friends of my family." See that? That's the reason why the viewership is skyrocketing. What's interesting is every person viewing "Catch a Contractor" has either been ripped off, lied to, stolen from, or they're looking for a potential contract. Because at the end, what do Adam and Skip do? They go through what to look for, what should be code, an ethical contract, and ultimately how not to be ripped off from a contractor. They let you know the Danger in their industry. They are protecting you from massive Danger to you and your family in the construction world.
"

"Danger" is an attention-grabbing word. It gets people to pay attention to you. USE IT! Your response to your marketing will skyrocket.

Word #14: Is This You?

This is Word #44 in the *57* Must Use Words in Every Piece of Marketing You Do for Your Business book.

This is definitely one of my favorites.

"Is this you, searching for a contractor you can trust, searching for a realtor you can trust?"

"It this you, dealing with dissatisfaction and frustration?"

"Is this you, buying every CD and DVD online in the world of self-help and motivation and still stuck in the same place?"

You ask them, "Is this you?" You get them thinking and they ultimately say, "That is me!" They raise their hand. Then you give them a free report and/or bonus information about your business, which starts to open up and develop the relationship between you and them. You let them know you don't cut any corners. "Is this you? Are you tired of your contractor not paying attention to you about your home renovation?"

Interesting! How simple yet powerfully effective the words tie all together!

What happens? Someone says, "Yes, it's me." They're listening to you. They're paying attention to you. How powerful is that? Developing a highly successful business is simply a result of being laser-focused on paying attention to what you say to your clients and also being strong enough to challenge them on what really is going on.

Word #15: Your Top *3* Words

This is a little different, because it's an exercise for you! Take your top *3* words that you learned in this teaching and own them in your business.

Use them. Get comfortable. Find your niche. Use them in your marketing. Use them in your words with your customers and colleagues. It's up to you which words you select.

Grab a hold of the three words and start to make them part of your marketing to change lives forever! This will take you to the level of getting uncomfortable, but you will truly enjoy marketing once you understand the lives you change by being truthful and honest. This is the powerful teaching to really elevate you in the power of having your customers, clients, patients, or consumers listening to you.

Absolutely FREE *57* Must Use
Marketing Words for You!
www.FreeMarketingWords.com

Remember that the average person right now is not being listened to in their personal life. How many of you have had to say to someone, "Would you listen to me, please?" We're used to saying that in our relationship life – not our marketing life – "Would you please listen to me?"

You must understand that people are so used to not being paid attention to or listened to in their everyday lives that you have to give them a reason to pay attention to you in business. As a marketer, you must show them attention and get them to listen to you plus you must listen to them. The more you listen and the more you learn about your customers, the more you will engage long-term relationships.

Listen, learn, grabbed their attention with your marketing words, and your customers will start paying attention to you. More importantly, your business will absolutely explode!

Now, choose your top *3* words and start to own them!

John: Everyone say it with me, "I speak less. I use these words more effectively, and I get comfortable with understanding my role as a marketer, which is to change lives!"

Coaching Students: I speak less. I use these words more effectively, and I get comfortable with understanding my role as a marketer, which is to change lives!

John: Now that was an awesome teaching!

To find out more about John Di Lemme and how you can achieve success in every area of your life and business, visit www.LifestyleFreedomClub.com.

You may also Call or Text (561) 847-3467 to speak with one of John's Elite, Record-Breaking team members.

Absolutely FREE *57* Must Use Marketing Words for You!
www.FreeMarketingWords.com

www.ingramcontent.com/pod-product-compliance
Lightning Source LLC
Chambersburg PA
CBHW072249170526
45158CB00003BA/1041